PREVIOUS PUBLICATIONS

Thoughts Feelings Visions Memories
How to Survive on a Little
I'll Wait
Love Has No Color
The Pirates Who Found Jesus
Joe's Most Dangerous Mission
(Sequel to I'll Wait)
Who Did It?

THOUGHTS OF
MIND

DORIS M. JONES

Trafford rev. 06/21/2019

 www.trafford.com

North America & international
toll-free: 1 888 232 4444 (USA & Canada)
fax: 812 355 4082

PART I

GENERAL
POEMS

CONTENTS

WHEN I AM OLD

When I am old and mentally deranged

Handle me with care and not like I am strange

When I call, please answer with kindness

For I am old and absent mindless

Remember me when I was young and able to stand

Don't pull away from me, hold my hand

Love me with the same tenderness and strength

As you did when I still had good sense

The Lord has let me live into old age

Please don't put me away in a cage

Remember my face and beautiful smile

That you enjoyed so much as a child

I am the same woman who gave birth to you And was
there with love your life through

STILL THE SAME

You once looked upon my face

   As if I were the queen of grace

      Your hand gently stroked my breast

        As you lay your head on my chest

You smiled at me as I to you

   And promised each other our love true

      Many years have passed up by

        And we pledged our love until we die

Time has not let us forget who we are

   And that we are still the same so far

      Although, it was long ago that we met,

        With each other we shall remain with

          no regret

2

You now look upon my face

As if I were the queen of grace

Your hand gently stroke s my breast

As your head lay on my chest

COLOR IS OBSOLETE

Children knows no color in what they do

They are very innocent and sincere too

Children can meet for the first time

And for them, there is no color line

They will laugh and hug each other

It doesn't matter the color of their Mother

To a child, color doesn't matter, it's obsolete

Surround them with other children and they

are complete

AUTUMN

Leaves are falling to the ground

There is so much beauty all around

Children are playing here and there

And anxious to go to the Autumn Fair

Some children with a smiling face

That puts joy all over this place

The wind blowing a whispering song

That will last all Autumn long

The trees are brown and bare

And there are leaves everywhere

Everything is quiet and still

Except the children who are thrilled

Autumn often bring dark and rainy days

But they are enjoyable in many ways

DON'T CRY

Don't cry for me when I am gone-I am in your heart and you are not alone

My love will always be with you-and remember the things that we used to do

When you think of me, put a smile on your face-and thank God for His loving grace

He brought us a mighty long way-and protected us each and every day

God put us together for the time that we had-just thank Him from your heart and don't be sad

We shared a love like no other-and no matter what, I will always be your Mother

Time will come and slowly pass you by-and one day we will be together again, so don't you cry

MY MOTHER'S BED

My Mother is gone but when I lay on her bed-I feel a loving peace that flows from my toes to my head

There is comfort when I am in pain-although I know that I will never see her again

Just to lie on her bed gives me a peace of mind-no matter what the problem is, I know that I will be fine

Lying on my Mother's bed brings me great joy and peace-and all my troubles seem to cease

The sense of where she used to be-makes me feel safe and trouble free

Lying on my Mother's bed is the best place for me-since her death, this is where I feel security

THE SEAGULLS

The seagulls glitter in the sky

Flying high and wide as they go by

They have their own formation

As they fly to their destination

They seem to enjoy what they do

As they gather and fly through

Some are in rows of six or nine

While some are following behind

They sway, dip and dive away

As they flutter and joyfully play

They are a beautiful sight in the sky

As the evening slowly draws nigh

The seagulls continue their formation

And never lose sight of their destination

THE CLOUDS

Planes fly above the clouds in the sky

They are so beautiful that I could cry

Nestled together with God's grace

Standing in the atmosphere of space

Some clouds slowly floats away

And as they travel, they shift and sway

God's creation is so awesome to see

As they float across the sky so freely

The clouds form shapes as they are sizing

Some are unique and very surprising

In the awesome forms that they take

And the creative designs that they make

UNCLE CHARLIE

We have been talking long distance for a year-and I hold our friendship and conversations very dear

It was many years ago that we met-but your face, my memory did not forget

Aunt Lela would cook dinner and we came to eat-then we sat and talked after such a treat

This is to wish you, Happy 86th Birthday-with good happiness and health, I pray

I know that you, miss Aunt Lela very much-just remember her love and gentle touch

Uncle Charlie, you are a very gentle man-full of humor and strength to withstand

I thank God for knowing the both of you-and I will remember our times together my life through

YOUR MOM

Your Mom has gone to her heavenly place

Don't fret, just remember her beautiful face

I know the pain seems hard to bare

But she's God's child and in His care

There will be days of pain and sorrow

Remember things will be better tomorrow

Cry if you must but let it be joy

She's in God's hands, the Devil can't destroy

Your Mom is out of misery and pain

And when it's time, you will see her again

Treasure all the beautiful memories of love

And thank your heavenly Father above

For all those years that she was here

With her in your heart, she is always near

MY LAS VEGAS TRIP

It has been many years since I was here

But memories I made, I will hold dear

Being with family is number two in my life

I enjoyed being with my son, grandson and his wife

It was hot when outside in the heat

And their friends were many to meet

We had plenty of food and time together.

And no one was concerned about the weather

My trip was one in the last few years

I thank God it wasn't sad or full of tears

A pleasure trip it was and I hope more to come

To enjoy family and have lots of fun

A HANKERCHIEF OF LOVE

Over the last few years-you have shed many tears. For adult and childhood pain-and you felt that you couldn't be happy again.

You can't seem to let God and let go-so you won't suffer any mo. I am here with a hankerchief of love- with blessings from our Father above.

I can wipe away your tears-and make you happy for the rest of your years. Stop loving me for one day and the next, you push me away.

Trust God to put it in the past-so you can enjoy happiness at last. I love you now and tomorrow-and will love your through your sorrow.

I have a hankerchief of love for you-that can bring joy in your life if you want it too. Don't push me and my love way-because I am going to love you forever and a day.

THE KEY TO YOUR HEART

You said you will give me the key to your heart. I will gladly lock myself in so that we will never part.

My love will be with your ever heart beat I will love you from your head to your feet. Together, we will always be- Sharing our love until eternity

The key to your heart is mine to keep- You will love me and we will have peace We will enjoy each other in love- And thank our heavenly Father above

For allowing us to meet and be together-To share our love forever

LOOK BEYOND YOUR PAIN

Look beyond your pain-because when you do you will see happiness again.

Don't focus on previous tribulations-because it's a new dawn and a new day for you to focus on our relation.

The years are passing you by-you don't have time to waste, sit or cry.

Embrace and love me true-and I will always be faithful and love you.

Sometimes the greater love comes late in years- so enjoy, be happy for there is no time for tears.

You can't erase anything that happened in the past but you can put it to rest at last.

SOME LOVE FROM DAD

A boy is not as delicate as a woman or girl but he needs to know that he is loved in this world

He needs a hug and kiss every now and then, so he can feel like his Dad is his friend

A boy needs love and attention too-just like his Mother and his sister do

Some love from Dad will do him well-by the way he carries himself, you can tell

Some love from Dad is all he needs-To make him to want to do good deeds

Boys are often quiet and shy-But when they get hurt, they sometimes cry

All a boy needs for his Dad to say-I love you each and every day

And I will be there to love and guide you-During your experiences your life through

THROUGH MY WINDOW

Through my window I see nature at its' best

And I see a bird in a tree building his nest

I see the rain as it hits the large trees

Then I see big and small falling leaves

Through my window I see the seasons change

And sometimes the weather seems strange

There are many different things in sight

And all are not of joy and delight

Through my window is like a town event

Of people's lives and some without a cent

Some have families, jobs and homes to go to

But some are homeless and don't know what to do

LISTEN TO YOUR PARENTS

Youthful years for some, are hard to bare

Thinking that your parents don't care

Feeling that you are grown and can do just

Not realizing that obeying your parents is a must

Thinking that you know it all

Can make the tallest feel small

Parents do the very best that they can

To teach you how to become a woman

or man

Giving you the love that you need

And setting a foundation to help you

Succeed in life, be patient and go slow

Don't be one to follow the flow

THE DAY THAT I DIED

On September 17, 2017, I woke up with blood coming out of my nose

It was flowing so fast that I got nervous from my head to my toes

I pinched the tip of my nose and held it very tight-but the blood coming out of my mouth was an ugly sight

Since I could tell that the flow wasn't going to stop, I told my grandson Thomas that I have to see a doc

We got in his car and he was driving a hundred miles an hour-I told him to slow down before we get a flat tire All I could think of was if we had a blowout-that our lives would be over without a doubt

God blessed us to make it safely to the Riverside Community Hospital Emergency Room-by then the bleeding was slowing down and would stop soon

After being there for a while, we heard a call for Code Blue-I prayed for that person and their family too

Later there was another Code Blue call-so I prayed again that God would bless them all

In my IV I was given Hydralazine to bring my blood pressure down —afterwards I told the Doctor that I was feeling faint

As I looked around, the Doctor lowered my bed and put the oxygen mask over my face-the last thing I remember was my body relaxing in grace

When I was coming back, my mind was blank. I heard a Nurse shout, "The numbers are coming up! The numbers are coming up! I had no fear but I knew that I was not alone because Jesus was near

When I opened my eyes, I was smiling and I said loudly, "I've got Jesus! They all started laughing and one of them said, "She's got Jesus." And they laughed again.

That was the day that I died and Jesus brought me back alive!

Note*God brought me back so I would know that He did it and not the Code Blue Team. They didn't get to touch me. This was God's glory! Thank you Jesus! This is true.

SPRING FLOWERS

Spring is here and flowers are everywhere, reminding us of Jesus presence and that He care.

He still loves and watches over us so in Him we must learn to trust.

Spring flowers bring freshness in the air. It's Jesus Christ who helps us in despair.

Spring flowers make everything look new and refreshed as the morning dew.

Jesus washes us as white as snow and He is the one we should get to know.

Spring flowers show us new life begins like when Jesus removes our sins.

Spring flowers are beautiful, to smell and see, just like the beauty of Jesus in you and me.

LIFE CYCLE

Aging is a normal part of life's cycle and a natural process of gaining respect-that brings psychological changes, wisdom and service that should not cause shame or regret.

While age brings diminishing strength and feeble mindness some grow weary and foolish and absent mindless.

But God's grace and mercy is forever the same-even if they don't remember their own name.

Although some began to walk tired and slow-but they remember Jesus name wherever they go.

Their sight slowly fades away-but they still get on their knees and pray.

POPPA HENDERSON

Poppa was a man of character, nice and funny-He could pray and make any gloomy day sunny

He was a man in love with Jesus Christ-and would tell you to give Him your life

Poppa always spoke of Jesus-no matter what he had to say, stay with Jesus and let Him guide your way

He was a man with a beautiful spirit and smile-he often said, Church stay with Jesus, He's coming back in a while

You have to stay with Jesus and His Word, please share with those who have not heard

Jesus is coming to take us all home one day, so each morning when you awake, don't forget to pray

Poppa loved all the songs that were played but when he heard oo-wee, he stood, smiled and swayed

OUR JOURNEY

We all will travel different roads and avenues- because as we go through life, we must pay our dues

As time goes on, our trials and tribulations will appear Sometimes they disrupt our lives and leave us in fear

As we journey farther into this life of ours, we must realize that we live by God's powers

Instead of trusting in God and letting Him do His work, we want to reinvent the wheel and stay on this useless trek

Man was given certain knowledge and wisdom but thinks he knows it all. When he realizes he's made a mess of things, it is God, he calls.

IF I LIVE TO GET OLD

If I live to get old-I pray that you won't treat me cold

Please be loving and kind to me-And don't make me feel less humanly

Some days will be good for me-And some will make me sad, you see

Growing old and being left alone-makes you feel that you want to leave and go home

Just be nice and become a friend of mine-because it does not take a lot to be kind

Some say old folk are just a headache-The truth is, that's a mistake

I only want to be treated nice and fair-And know that my family care

I will do my best to work with you-If you will be courteous in all you do

LIKE A ROLLING STONE

We live our lives on a merry-go-round-as we find ourselves tumbling up and down.

We all are lost like a rolling stone-who sometimes find ourselves sad and alone.

Often wondering what tomorrow may hold-and letting our lives get out of control.

We roll from one avenue to another-in search of our father and mother.

A rolling stone rolls all by itself-and in its' path there is nothing left.

We warble. twist, tumble and turn-and for many earthly things, we yearn.

We must stop tumbling and rolling around and realize that God's gift for us is sound.

There is no need to be roaming like a bee because His mercy and grace has set us free.

TEENAGERS

Having teenagers in the house

May be worse than having a mouse

All the food seems to disappear

And nobody knows why it's not here

They like to play their music loud

And wonder why you have to shout

Teenagers don't like to get up

And get angry when you have to fuss

When you let them drive the car

They are late because they went too far

Some friends they took home

They were suppose to be in the car alone

PART II

INSPIRATIONAL POEMS

CONTENTS

A LITTLE TALK WITH JESUS

When I woke up this morning, I heard a voice that said, "You have planned many things and you have a choice. What will you do today before you go your way? Will you take time to thank me for waking you? Or will you continue on the way you do?"

I realized that the voice I heard was coming from my Lord. As I looked around, I said, "Forgive me God. Let your Angels stay and protect me, as you guide my life and set me free."

"Now I realize that I have been neglecting you, so I will work on reading your word and sharing it too. A little talk with Jesus is what I need each day and to thank God for blessings me as I pray."

JESUS IS THE LIGHT

Jesus is the light that I need each day

Jesus is the light that guides me on my way

Jesus is the light that shines all the time

Jesus is the light that helps keep my mind

Jesus is the light that shines everywhere

Jesus is the light that holds me in His care

Jesus is the light that gives me hope for tomorrow

Jesus is the light when I have sorrow

Jesus is the light that will forever shine

Jesus is the light that will forever be mine

MY BLESSINGS

For over twenty-five years I have suffered with a lot of pain from a fall-But when the pain is severe, God let me know that He hears my call.

I have many ups and downs but can still put a smile on my face-Because I will not let pain and agony stop me from running this race.

God has been so good to me that it is beyond all measure-He has eased my pain many times-So in life I could have some pleasure.

There have been many nights that God showed me His glory-And it reminded me of Jesus' story. Remembering the suffering and pain that

Jesus had to endure-Made me realize that what I'm going through is not great because there is a cure.

I thank God each and every day for the good and the bad-Because I am not exempted from tribulations that will make me sad.

I thank God for the pain that wracks my body at night-He always gives me some relief Because He is the one that has the power and might.

SPIRITUAL OVERHAUL

Lord, wash me as white as snow and give me a new and clean heart-So I will know the way to go to serve you and never part.

Cleanse me in the blood of your Son so that I will have a renewed mind-Because in this race I want to run to my heavenly Father who is kind.

Lord, give me the spirit to do the things that you command of me-So I will learn to believe and trust you-Then I can receive my blessing from thee.

Engrave your words in my heart so I will love my sisters and brothers-The way you wanted me from the start-to share your word with all others.

Lord, give me a total new walk so others may see you in me-As I go about my day and talk of the trials and tribulations that must be.

I thank you Lord for saving my soul and giving me a mind to repent-So one day I can walk the streets of gold and everyone will know where I went.

THANK YOU LORD

Thank you Lord for the sunshine-thank you for the rain. Thank you for the wind-thank you for the pain.

As I awake each day I want to thank you for my sight-Thank you for showing me the way and loving me with all your might.

I want to thank you for my bed and the warm covers at night-Thank you for a roof over my head and for letting me know what is right.

Each day I thank you for your mercy and a whole new day of grace-Thank you for a man of clergy to teach me how to run this race.

Lord thank you for the plans for my life and giving me a chance to reconcile with you-Because your Son, you did sacrifice so I will know your word is true.

Thank you for the pains, headaches, trials and tribulations I must go through-For a chance to correct my mistakes and to give praise and glory to you.

SURROUNDED BY GOD

We are surrounded by God, he is everywhere-He is there because he loves us and care. His presence is like a flicker of light- And those who trust his word walk upright

We are surrounded each and every day-He is always near to guide us on our way. God is a Spirit but yet you can feel-His presence and you know that he is real

He is like a tall hovering tower–To protect us with his strength and power. God constantly shields us from harm-By extending his outstretched arm.

We live by God's mercy and loving grace-Even though we are not worthy to see his face. He's loving and kind to us-And he just asks that we believe and trust.

We are surrounded by God and all of his glory-Read your Bible and you will know the story.

EYES OF THE LORD

The eyes of the Lord are in every place-As he protects us
while we run this race

He is beholding the evil and the good-To help us do the
right things that we should

Our heavenly Father protects us from all harm-When
danger is near he stretches out his arm

When we are in pain in the middle of the night-There are
things we must endure that don't seem right

God knows what we are going through and our story-But
this is so we can tell others and give him the glory

There are trials and tribulations that we must bear-As did
our Saviour on the cross because he care.

The eyes of the Lord are in every place-And we should
thank Him each day for His mercy and grace

Jesus is the name that each and every one of us will call-
Just get on your knees and tell him all

The pain and problems that you are going through-And
he will whisper, "It's alright, I've got you."

A DAY TO REMEMBER

A day to remember was when Jesus came into my life, the pain that I felt when I realized his sacrifice.

The terrible beatings, agony and humiliation he went through-To save sinful people like me and you.

Tears from my eyes like a river flows-Brings joy knowing one day I will meet him and my heart glows.

Oh but I can visualize the pain on the cross-That he was willing to suffer to save the lost.

A day to remember when Jesus came into my life-His Word and teachings showed me how to live with no strife.

He showed me how to love my sisters and brothers-And to share his Word with family and others.

I must have faith in him and in all that I do-Because he felt it was worth rescuing me, knowing that my heart was true

He is my Saviour and guiding light-And I love him with my heart and all my might

I love him much more than a friend-Because he will always be with me until the end

THANKS I GIVE

Oh Lord, I want to see your face-so I can thank you for your loving grace

You gave me a new path to walk each day- with new mercies to carry me on my way

Thank you for your strength and guiding light-Lord to see your face is going to be a delight

You show me the way to go-And your word teaches me what I should know

You have given your Son to erase my sin-and you promised to be with me until the end

Each day that I awake with a new breathe of air-lets me know that you love me and care

Thank you for this race that I am here to run-And for the protection from the Holy Spirit and your Son

MOUNTAINS' BEAUTY

The Mountains are beautiful and high-They look like they can touch the sky

With a river of water flowing by-Seeing the beauty of it, you just sigh

God made the earth a beautiful place-And that shows His loving grace

The Mountains stand out by themselves-And God can't be out done by anyone else

He is majestic and has all power-That He uses to protect us every hour

His Mountains are grayish and rough-But they have a beauty that nothing can touch

DON'T GIVE UP ON YOUR DREAMS

No matter what you want to do in life-there will be trials, tribulations and sacrifice.

Set a long-term goal and pray-that you will fully suffice one day.

Ask God to guide and hold your hand-because He is the one who has your life planned.

Don't give up on your dreams-but you may have to revise your scheme.

No matter how old you are or what people say-stay in your lane and pray.

Sometimes your dreams will seem out of reach-but stay focused and don't get weak.

Jesus is on the main line-all you have to do is call Him sometime.

He hears every one of your prayers and call-and He will be there to pick you up when you fall.

Don't think you are too old and can't do-put your trust in Jesus and He will surprise you.

Don't give up on your dreams because of what others say-there are some who don't want to see you prosper any way.

Let God be your strength and high tower-He's the one who has all power.

Live your life with God and He will see you through-and let your dreams come true.

Don't give up on your dreams no matter what you do-you must persevere no matter what you go through.

One day you will realize that your dreams are one step up the ladder-and what you have gone through won't matter.

Keep pressing forward and keep your dreams in mind-they will come true because God is always on time.

Your trials and tribulations prepared you-for your dreams to come true.

A MOTHER'S PRAYER

A Mother's prayer is a powerful petition-she prays to God as her child goes through transition. God hears her every word and every cry-and He lets her know that He is standing by.

There are trials and tribulations that a child must go through-but a Mother knows when her prayer to God is due. God hears her every word and sees every tear-and He lets her know that He is always near.

Sometimes she wonders if He hears her call-but He is the one who picks up her child when they fall. A Mother's prayer lasts for many years-through the heartaches and many tears.

She knows God is her only help-so she prays for her child and herself. One day that child finally turns around- then she knows that God has picked her child up off the ground.

A Mother's prayer is powerful to be heard —and her loving Father hears every word.

WE HAVE TO TRUST GOD

We have to trust God in our darkest hour-He's the one who has all the power.

There is no one else that we can turn to-God is our everything and is always true.

He's there when things for us go wrong-loving and trusting Him keeps us strong.

God is our Father and heavenly light-no matter where we are, we are in His sight.

Storms may rage to and fro in our life-but all we have to do is surrender and turn to Christ.

God loves and care for all of us-He just wants us to give Him praise and trust.

We have to trust God because there is no one else-because we can't do what He can for our-self.

God is omniscient and He is our strong tower-and watches over us each and every hour.

JESUS IS BEHIND YOU

Be aware of the things that you say and do-

because Jesus is right behind you.

Treat people with great respect and love-and

thank God for your blessings from above.

Be kind to each and every one-so in you, they

will see the love of God's Son.

Jesus is right behind you-so be careful for all the

things you do.

Always give Him praise and glory-and read the

Bible, so you will know His story.

MAKE ME NEW

I am a sinner Lord, wash me, make me new-and smell as fresh as the morning dew.

Direct my feet wherever I go-and make me as white as snow.

Let your light shine in me-and others will know that I serve thee.

God gave His only begotten Son-now I will serve the Almighty One.

I will repent so I will be forgiven of my sin-so I can live an abundant life until the end.

Then I will welcome that glorious day-when Jesus come to take me away.

To my heavenly home, I will go-as I shine and glitter as the white snow.

My soul will be with my Father above-and I will rest for eternity in His love.

DON'T WORRY ABOUT TOMORROW

Don't worry about tomorrow or things to come-God is already there and watching to protect you from harm.

He knows your every need and hear your cry-just know that He is already there and standing by.

Don't waste your time and energy-God's power is strong and a mystery.

He has promised to never leave nor forsake us-all you have to do is just believe and trust.

Don't worry about things of tomorrow-God is always there to ease your worst sorrow.

Remember when you pray, God is never late-He is always on time, be patient and wait.

IF YOU FOLLOW JESUS

There will be many trials and tribulations of life-and many things you will have to sacrifice.

There will be persecution and anger toward you-but you must read the Word and do what it says to do.

Some things will happen that you won't understand-just remember for your life, God has a plan.

God is in control and sits on the throne-and you must know that you can't do anything on your own.

If you follow God, you will stand out-and be mistreated and there is no doubt.

If they hated Jesus, you know that they are going to hate you. So be prepared to follow God the way He wants you too.

AFTER A DEATH

After a close love one dies-You have a lot of pain and cries

There are a lot of things to prepare-And you sometimes end up in despair

The hurt penetrates deep inside-And with a love one, you confide

You think of all the memories past-And know that the pain will not last

There is a night for the wake-To review the body and correct mistakes

You go on preparing for that final day-And try to stay strong as you pray

You can't believe that they are gone-But life goes on and you must stay strong

You will never again, hear their voice-When the time comes, there is no choice

CELEBRATE JESUS

At Christmas we celebrate, praise and sing

To give glory to Jesus Christ our King

Peach on earth, love to all and mercy mild

So that God and sinners can be reconciled

During the year we forget how great God is

And that all we are and have is His

Giving all the honor, glory and praise

Is deserving for Jesus who rose from the grave

Light and life to man, God brings

And Jesus has risen with healing in His wings

He gave His life so man wouldn't die

As He laid His glory by

We sing Hail to Jesus' birth

Hoping to have peace on this earth

MY GOD

My God wakes me each morning and guides me during the day-but before I start, I take time to pray

Lord, I thank you for guiding and directing my life-nothing that I do or give will be greater than your sacrifice

Your Son, Jesus Christ died on a hill called Calvary-He died for the sins of the world and for me

My God, the Lord watches over me through the day-so I find a few moments here and there to pray

To give Him thanks for His mercy and grace-and waiting one day to see Him face to face

His immeasurable kindness is beyond all there is-and I appreciate it as I live

READ THE BIBLE

The Word of God judges the thoughts and attitudes of the heart.

We should prayerfully read God's Word before our day start.

There are many life instructions for us- if we will lean on Him and trust.

God is our heavenly Father who loves and care-He will not allow us to go through more than we can bare.

Let's come before the throne of grace-and pray that one day, we will see His face.

Jesus is God's only Son. By the Virgin Mary, He was born.

He came to earth to reconciliate God and man and to save and not desecrate.

He was crowned with honor and glory-read the Bible and learn that He is real and it tells His story.

GOD CAN DO IT BEST

Take your pain to the Alter because you need rest-let God handle it because this is what He does best.

He said come those who are laden with burdens-because I am your Father and I know what's best.

Stop worrying and trying to handle things yourself-you need rest because it's my job to take care of you because I know what's best.

Rely on me for your peace and rest-because I am the One who can do it best.

Give me your pain and worry less-I know what you need. I am your Father and I know what's best.

WE CAN'T GROW WITHOUT CHANGE

The trials and tribulations of life are to enhance our growth. If we don't experience changes in our lives, we cannot grow to the next level. This will cause stagnation and stunt our growth.

God's Word gives us all the spiritual power and nourishment that we need. We need to let it saturate our hearts and minds. On a daily basis, we need to read and meditate on God's Word so we can apply the principles to our lives.

The principles are the guidelines of God's promises. His promises are His guarantee that He will do whatever He say He will do. There is no growth if there is no change in our lives.

To have a personal relationship with God, we must grow so we can reach another level in lining our lives up with Him.

LORD, I WANT TO GLORIFY YOU

Lord, I want to glorify thy name in everything that I do and say-no matter how my life may change, I want to glorify you in every way.

Despite the trials and tribulations in my life, I want to be able to thank you. I want to give all the glory and praise to Jesus in everything that I do.

Lord, I want to glorify your name as I go about my walk each day. I thank you for being the same, no matter how far and long that I stray.

Lord, you are my guiding power and I know that you love me-because I have your protection every hour. I thank you for setting me free.

MY PROVIDER

Let the words of my mouth and the meditation of my heart-be acceptable in thy sight therefore I will never part

From you, Lord who watches over me-and gives me shelter and security

From those who want to harm me-and disrupt my life's destiny

But they forget that you are in control-and that I have given you, my life and my soul

Let me be at peace as they stumble and fall because when I need help, its' You, I call

You are my Provider and shield-from the enemy who wants to destroy and kill.

PROTECT YOURSELF

Put on your armor and your shield-and let the Lord protect you on the battlefield

The enemy is wicked and strong-but it's to the Lord that you belong

He will protect you from the firey darts-and all evil that comes toward your heart

Have faith and trust in Him-and watch what happens to them

The Lord is always watching over you-when the enemy attack He know what to do

He knew you before you were in your Mother's womb-and He will know you after you are in your tomb

You are forever and truly His-so your life you must sincerely give

He is your protection and shield-from those bullets on the battlefield

LORD, I THANK YOU

Lord, I thank you for this day-in everything that I do and say. Thank you for waking me in my right mind-and waking me one more time.

You are the head of my life-because your Son was the sacrifice. Lord, I thank you in all that I say-and will continually give you thanks and pray.

Thank you for guiding and directing my way-as I go about my routine each day. I thank you for Jesus Christ-and for His blood that cleansed my life.

Lord, I thank you for your loving grace-and I am looking forward to seeing your face. I love you in all that I do-and will serve you totally true.

WHO IS I AM?

I AM the one who spoke the world into existence. **I AM** the King of the world, your creator, your savior. **I AM** the beginning and the end. **I AM** Alpha and Omega, the first and the last. **I AM** the one who protects you from seen and unseen dangers.

I AM the one who loves you so much that that I gave my only begotten Son to die on Calvary for your sins.

I AM the one who wakes you each morning with new mercies and new grace. **I AM** the one who can give your troubled mind the peace that passes all understanding.

I AM your heavenly Father who gives you only good gifts. **I AM** the one who knows how many strands of hair are on your head. **I AM** the one who knew you before you were in your Mother's womb. **I AM** the Prince of Peace, the Lord of Lords and the King of Kings. **I AM that I AM!**

REMEMBER

As a Soldier away from home-just remember that you are not alone

Sometime the pain may be hard to bare-but remember God is with you and care

I know that at times you get lonely-but all you need is God's hands only

He will protect you day and night-you can't see Him but He has you in sight

Stay in prayer and hang touch-just remember God will be there when things get rough

Just trust Him with all your heart —you will know that He was with you from the start

WORD ENCOUNTER

A encounter is to assimilate the word into our heart...so we can be protected from our enemy's firey darts. The word is to give us directions and guidance for life and in return there will be some sacrifice.

We must go into our secret place with God each day-so we can get to know Him in an intimate way. God's Word is our protecting force-and the Bible is our only true source.

God's basic instructions before leaving earth-should be discerned for its' worth. The thief comes to steal, kill and destroy-but Jesus came so that we could have life more abundantly to enjoy.

He is the resurrection, the truth and the life-and God's only begotten Son who was the living sacrifice. Therefore, we need to get close enough to God to hear His Word-so we can share it with those who have not heard...

Our first ministry is to God alone-the Sovereign One who sits on the throne. We will be surprised by giving God the glory and what He will do through us...

If only in Him, we would learn to trust-God wants to give us glory so He can get the glory... and we need to read the Bible so we will know the story.

God wants us to be in His will-and that's for as long as we live. We are His children and His treasure. His love is so unlimited that we can't measure...

The height, width and depth of it or His mercy and grace...that He showers us with all over this place. The Word is to broaden our knowledge range...so we can make a complete life change.

INSPIRATION OF HEAVEN

Heaven is a place of beautiful scenery and a spiritual quietness.

There will be no cars, trucks or buses of any kind and no more noise and pollution.

The morning air will have the smell of a mixture of flowers and the morning dew.

Everyone will give and sing praises to God for all of His mighty blessings.

There will be no need to worry about food or water nor clothes or shoes.

The musical sound from all the different musical instruments will be appeasing to the ear.

No more hate or killing each other, nothing but love and joy.

But the most beautiful sound of all will be the voice of God saying, "A job well done, my good and faithful servant."

SATAN IS OUR ENEMY

Satan is dragging us away from Jesus...the only one who we can believe and trust

Pay attention to what is going on around you...read God's word so you will know what to do

The enemy's job is to steal, kill and destroy...if you are not careful he will rip you up like a toy

Trust and believe in God's holy word...and don't be afraid to share with those who haven't heard

Trust God with your whole heart and soul...and believe the Bible because that is His story is told

You must put God first in everything you do...because He is the only you can trust and is true

Don't let Satan drag you away from Christ... because he doesn't mean any good in your life

OUR DAILY ROUTINE

As we go about life, we have a daily routine that goes in a cycle that doesn't seem to end.

Everything that we do including the style of clothes we wear goes around in a circle and comes back with a different flare.

We go to our jobs each day and do the same thing, from summer, fall, winter and spring.

The sun goes down and rises up again as the wind blows around and blows the sand.

Every death is replaced with a new born, for there is really nothing new under the sun.

We laugh, smile and sometimes cry and sometimes we don't know why.

Through it all we manage to survive because we are human and is alive.

SHOWING GRACE

Since God shows me new mercies and grace, it makes me more determined to see His face.

Of all the trials and tribulations that I go through, I know God is on the throne and knows what to do.

He gives me the right amount of peace and knows exactly when to make my troubles cease.

God gives me new mercies and grace each day that I awake and the amount that I need, there is no mistake.

He blesses me over and over again so He can get me to the place of His plan.

He knows me inside out and I love Him and there is no doubt.

The Lord shows me grace in all kind of ways and strengthens my faith to keep me all of my days.

JESUS DIED AND ROSE AGAIN

Jesus hung and died on the cross to save the wicked and the lost

He shed His blood on the hill of Calvary to save wretched sinners like you and me

He can wash us clean and as white as snow and be with us wherever we go

Jesus is the Savior who died for us all to reconcile man and God after the fall

He came to earth and lived as a man and taught us the word so we would understand

That God has for our lives a plan and we must believe in Him to withstand

The attacks from our enemy which comes from everywhere, God will protect and keep us in His care

Jesus rose from the dead so that we may have eternal life and He wants us to love each other without strife.

OBEDIENCE IS IMPORTANT

When you think of Gods' law day and night, You can learn to live and do what's right

For only then will you succeed and God will definitely hear your plea

You must be bold and stay strong because when you obey you can't go wrong

Banishing fear and doubt from your mind you will realize that God is always on time

Being obedient to the word and God's law you will have prosperity and success with no flaw

Just remember God is with you wherever you go and is the best guide and protector that you know

HE DIED FOR US

Great is the Lord and greatly to be praised

He's the One our Savior, He raised

God will be our guide even until death

He died to save us from our-self

For all our sins, He hung on the cross

To save the evil, wicked and lost

They nailed His hands, His head hung high

Mary watched her child and did cry

But she knew that this had to be

To save sinners like you and me

Jesus is the only way to the Father above

And His death was showing us His love

GOD IS MY EVERYTHING

God is my refuge, salvation and glory

I live my life by His commandments in His story

He is my strength and my great rock

His hands the firey darts, He will block

The Lord has given us directions and laws

And in His commandments there are no flaws

He knows how He wants our lives to be

Because He has already set our destiny

He wants us to love and treat each other right

Because He loves us with all His might

BLACK HISTORY MONTH

We are celebrating a time where God has allowed us to advance. Reaching this point in history is not mere chance.

We have had many struggles and adversities to face but we made it through with God's grace.

There are still things we must endure but God is our Divine protection and that's for sure.

If we just trust Him and believe, His wonderful blessings we will receive.

Black History Month is a time to reflect that Black people deserve some respect.

We are all sisters and brothers in Christ and need to love each other in this life.

Jesus Christ gave His life for us all so we could have eternal life after the great fall.